CHRISTY PARK

Mario Mazzotta
A TEEN AND YOUNG ADULT MEMOIR
SHORT STORIES

"Christy Park," by Mario Mazzotta. ISBN 978-1-63868-164-9 (softcover); 978-1-63868-165-6 (ebook).

Published 2024 by Virtualbookworm.com Publishing Inc., P.O. Box 9949, College Station, TX 77842, US. ©2024, Mario Mazzotta. All rights reserved. No part of this publication may be reproduced, stored in a retrieval system, or transmitted in any form or by any means, electronic, mechanical, recording or otherwise, without the prior written permission of Mario Mazzotta.

CHRISTY PARK

A collection of true short stories (slightly embellished) about a first-generation American's "slice of life" remembrances growing up in a small blue-collar mill town outside of Pittsburgh during World War II.

The names of my friends, neighbors, teachers, and others have been changed.

"Hereby too, I indulge the inclination so natural in old men, talking of themselves and their own past actions."

Ben Franklin

Contents

1. Christy Park 1
2. Eleventh Ward Elementary School 5
3. Friend or Foe 11
4. Tony the Ragman 16
5. The Malocchio Lady 20
6. To Dib or Not to Dib 24
7. The Clark Bar and the Binoculars......29
8. Frannie...35
9. Little Robbie Cole.............................38
10. Bare-Ass Beach 43
11. Survival of the Fittest.....................47
12. The Resurrection 51
13. Amen..55
14. Paydays 64

15. THE FOREIGNER 69

16. THE FIGHT 76

17. S.L. 81

18. TECH OR VOC 87

EPILOGUE 93

AUTHOR'S NOTE 95

1.
CHRISTY PARK

Hi, my name is Mario.

When I was growing up my little world consisted of a blue-collar steel mill neighborhood outside of Pittsburgh known as Christy Park. I never knew how it got its name. Nobody by the name of Christy lived there. And it certainly didn't look like a park.

It had eight steep, vertical streets, numbered 24 through 31, each of which was connected horizontally by alleyways. The frame and shingled-roof houses that lined the streets all looked alike. They were "company" houses sold to our fathers by the U.S. Steel Company. Our fathers "came from the old country" and worked three different eight-hour shifts in the war-time (World War II) steel mills. They continued to eat their "old country" foods, drink home-made wine, and expected us to "study hard in school to get a good job." And, above all, we were constantly warned to "do nothing to shame the family name."

Each of the streets in the Park was dead-ended at the top by heavily-treed hillsides and at the bottom by a horizontal street named Walnut. Below Walnut Street were two sets of railroad tracks (with a tunnel underneath), then steel mills (U.S. Steel National Tube Works and Fort Pitt Steel & Foundry) bordering the flat banks of the Youghiogheny River. I wasn't sure how the Youghiogheny got its name either, but guessed it had something to do with Indians living in the Park before the steel mills came.

2

Christy Park had no church. But there were a lot of churches on the top of the hill above the Park, an area known as Grandview, where the rich people lived. There was no steel mill in Grandview and it was easy to guess how it got its name.

Christy Park had no library, not even in our elementary school. But our teachers told us there was a "big library" in Grandview.

Nor did it have a public swimming pool. But, you guessed it, Grandview had one.

What Christy Park did have was kids. Tons of them. Most families had three or four. The Santucci family had the most---eight. My friend Augie was one of them. My other friends were Enzo, who was my best friend, Alfrado, and Squirt. We all lived on 25th Street. Like our houses we all looked alike---dark wavy hair, light-tan skin, brown eyes, pretty-big noses, skinny frames, and average height, except Squirt, who, as his nickname suggested, was on the shorter side.

Our playground consisted of the Yough, railroad tracks, streets, alleys, porches, and the treed hillsides. We swam in the Yough in the summer and walked across it when frozen solid in the winter. We hopped the boxcars of freight trains to ride downtown to see Saturday Tarzan movie-matinees for 25 cents, played tag football, basketball and baseball on the level bottom part of our street, sneaked in some innocent boy-girl stuff in the dark alleys, slept on porches on hot summer nights, and built secret clubhouse shacks in the hillside.

Christy Park---my little world and I loved it.

2.
Eleventh Ward Elementary School

I don't remember much from my early years at Eleventh Ward Elementary School, a public school at the top of 29th Street in the Park. The school was a one-story cement-block building with a principal's office, 8 classrooms, and a boy's and girl's bathroom. Nothing else, except an adjoining flat-surfaced cement area where we were ushered out by the teachers to play at recess.

Here is what I remember:

- All of the teachers were women---who really cared about us learning.

- A note to my mom and dad from my first-grade teacher, Miss Taylor, asking them not to speak in Italian to me at home.

- Our first-grade "Reader", a pretty colored picture book about a young boy and girl named Dick and Jane and a cute dog named Spot. None of us kids could relate to most of it. In fact, my friend Squirt said his dad called it a "Grandview" book.

- Homework had to be first completed and checked by my mom before going out to play after school.

- Gold or green stars on my report cards.

- Breakfasts of Mother's Oats in the winter and Corn Flakes in the warmer months.

- A pair of new clodhopper shoes at the beginning of each school year.

- The long walk to the top of my street and then four more blocks through unpaved alleyways to school. Home for lunch, and then back to school. Sun, rain, or snow---no school buses for anyone.

- Frozen water pipes in our house on some winter mornings. No water---not a drop to drink.

- A home-made necklace of garlic cloves on a string and worn to school (out of sight under my T-shirt) on freezing winter days to prevent colds.

- Saturday night baths in a metal wash-tub on the kitchen floor, near the stove, where water was heated in a large pot and poured into the tub. Elbows and knees scrubbed with black "Lava" soap that felt like sandpaper.

- Tony Bianchi wetting his pants "after recess" while sitting at his desk. How was that possible after bathroom recess? Well, our 2nd grade teacher, Miss Stickrath, who was a stickler for rules, was so upset Tony played during recess ("I don't need to go") that she wouldn't give him permission to go after returning to our classroom. Tony cried after he peed, but lucky him, he got to go home from school early.

- The school nurse's note to my parents stating that I had head lice. And my hair smelling strongly of vinegar the next couple of days at school.

- Classroom spelling bee contests, girls standing on one side of the room, boys standing on the other, having to sit if you misspell a word, with girls always winning.

- Boys getting paddled in the cloakroom for not doing their homework.

- A "Good Citizenship" pamphlet awarded to the student of each class who purchased the most 10 cents war-bond stamps. With Gilbert Goldberg the year-after-year winner of my class.

- Blue and Gold Stars displayed in the front windows of homes throughout the Park. The blue star signified a father or son was serving in the war and the gold star signified that a member of the family was killed in action.

- I do remember 5th grade more clearly. I was both scared and anxious to face Miss Benson, the school's toughest and best teacher. Only two or three students made her honor roll.

And no more easy subjects. She taught courses in geography, history, science, literature, and problem-solving math, with tons of homework every night. I still remember her clever history memory drills, such as, "PPPizarro went to PPPeru and Cortezzz went to Mexxxico." And her telling us to remember that we have our HOMES in the United States--- HOMES---being a word clue for recalling the names of the Great Lakes. I will never forget Miss Benson---she was the first teacher to stir the grey matter in my head.

- And, finally, the best part: celebrating the end of each school year with fun-filled family picnics and roller coaster rides at Kennywood Amusement Park.

That's it for the early school years.

3.
FRIEND OR FOE

Saturday afternoon during the fall months meant football. Nearly all the kids who lived on the street participated.

Our field: the level cement pavement at the bottom of our street. Each team consisted of four players: a center, a quarterback, and two receivers. Game after game was played, with the losing team dropping out, until one team was left to claim the victory trophy---bragging rights for the week at Eleventh Ward Elementary School.

One Saturday's game ended unexpectedly when our tightly-wound, rubber-banded, home-made paper football rolled down and into the corner sewer before any of us could grab it.

On our way home, Enzo complained that he was sick and tired of playing with a fake football. "I have a plan," he said "next Saturday, let's try to play with the rich kids on the hill."

Early next Saturday morning, Enzo and I took the path up to the top of the hill to Grandview, where the rich kids lived.

"Friend or foe" shouted two boys who were playing pitch and catch with a real football.

"What's a foe?" Enzo whispered to me. Ignoring Enzo's question, I shouted "We're friends, can we play too?"

After an hour or so of tossing and catching a real ball, a mother called one of the boys to "come home." As soon as he went into his house, Enzo worked his plan. "Nice catch," he said to the other kid. "Now let's see if you can catch a long pass." Then, as soon as the kid turned his back and started to run a long pass pattern, Enzo headed over the hill with the football. I quickly followed. We didn't stop running until we reached the bottom of the hill where we felt safe.

That Saturday afternoon, for the first time EVER, we played with a real football.

The next morning after church, I asked Enzo, "Did you think the ball was worth stealing? I didn't sleep much last night."

"Neither did I," he said. "But, I didn't really steal it, I just borrowed it to see how it would feel to play with a real ball."

"Well how did it feel?"
"Not any more fun than when we play with our home-made ball."

"Yeah, I agree," I said "let's hurry up and return it before Mr. Hackett, the juvenile officer, knocks on our door and we end up in reform school like poor Jerome Rizzo."

So, we hurried up the path to the top of the hill, placed the football by the front door of the rich kid's porch, and left a note:

"I guess we were foes. Sorry."

***

PAPER FOOTBALL RECIPE

1. Gather about 15 pages of newspaper.
2. Stack the pages on a flat surface.
3. Carefully and neatly fold the pages over and over until you reach a size approximately 6 inches in length.
4. Tightly roll the width-end of the paper into a cylinder. When this step is finished, the width of the cylinder should be about 3 inches.

5. On each end of the cylinder, place a thick homemade rubber band cut from an inner tube.
6. Soak the cylinder in a bucket of water overnight.
7. Remove in the morning and set outside to dry.
8. After the cylinder hardens, your homemade football is ready for action.

4.
TONY THE RAGMAN

It was summer and Enzo and I were playing mumble-peg on my front porch when we spotted Tony passing by. He was heading home.

Tony was a small man who was always dressed the same way: a much too-big black overcoat, layered over a shirt buttoned at the collar, long pants, leather work shoes, and a dingy-black tassel cap pulled down over his ears. He looked old and tattered and so did his clothes. As usual, he was carrying his Balsamo shopping bag filled with all sorts of rags.

"Hi, Tony," we shouted from the porch. As always, Tony nodded his head slightly to say "Hi" back to us kids. And, as always, he never stopped to speak. He just kept shuffling up 25th Street to his home, a small windowless tar paper shack, deep in the woods above the last row of houses at the top of the street. No one knew when or who built his home. It just appeared one day. Just like Tony.

We kids had a lot of questions about Tony: Where did he come from? How old was he? Did he have any family? Was he in the war? Where does he go every day? Where does he get all those rags? What does he do with them? Lots of questions. No answers.

He was pure mystery in Christy Park, a neighborhood where everyone knew everyone and everything about everyone. Yet, no one even knew Tony's last name. Mr. Santucci's house was the closest to Tony's so he stopped him one evening and told him that he could take anything to eat from his garden anytime he wanted. Then he asked him his name and was told simply "Tony." Mr. Santucci did not pry any further.

Nor did our mothers and fathers help clear things up. They told each of us kids pretty much the same thing. Our fathers: "Leave him alone." "Don't bother him." "He doesn't bother anybody." "Nothing to worry about, he wouldn't harm a flea." And so forth. Our mothers: "Don't tease him or make fun of him, or you'll have to confess it to Father Rossi." "Be nice to him." "Pray for him at mass." And so forth. Lots of advice. No answers.

And so, year after year, the Balsamo bag went down 25th Street in the morning and went back up the street before nightfall.

Then one day it happened.

Tony the Ragman died. News of his death flashed up and down the streets of the Park. The police found him dead at his home on a make-shift bed of old rags.

I was swinging on the porch glider when Enzo yelled from the sidewalk below. "Hey Mair, did you hear the news?"

"Yeah, I know, Tony the Ragman is dead."

"No, not that news," said Enzo. "I mean the latest news, that Tony the Ragman was a woman."

5.
THE MALOCCHIO LADY

I remember it well. It was a sunny June afternoon and Enzo and I were playing Batman and Robin in my back yard. We had bath-towel capes around our necks and were lying on the top of my dad's corrugated tin garage roof when Robin, I mean Enzo, spotted a mysterious stranger walking through the alley behind the garage. The stranger was dressed totally in black and carried a small black suitcase. She walked through the back gate of my yard, along the side of the garage, up the path to the back porch steps, and disappeared into my house.

We were curious but not enough to stop playing. But, after rescuing a screaming widow from her burning house (our third heroic save of the day), we suddenly stopped playing when Enzo said, "Let's go see what's going on with that stranger lady." As usual, he was reading my mind.

We parachuted off the roof, ran to the back screen door, walked quietly through the kitchen, and listened at the bottom of the stairway leading up to the bedrooms. We couldn't make out what was being said and we also couldn't see anything. So we quietly took off our shoes, crept up the stairway and sat on the top of the stairs, looking down the hallway into my parent's bedroom. The window shades were drawn and the room was dimly lit by candles. The Jesus crucifix that hung on the wall over my parent's bed was now in the stranger's hands and she was slowly circling my seated mother uttering prayer-like chants. We heard my mother say: "No, I don't know who it could have been." "Yes, for over a year now." Then more praying out loud by the stranger who also was spraying something misty into the air. The hallway started to smell like the high-mass at St. Perpetua Church.

"This is boring" whispered Enzo "and a little weird, let's go." I agreed so we sneaked back down the steps and went back outside.

The next day Enzo had all the answers. His mom knew the mysterious lady. "Everyone knows of her even though she doesn't live in Christy Park. She is called the 'malocchio' lady."

"The what lady?" I asked.

"The malocchio lady. My mom told me that she a special relationship with God who gives her the power to remove a spell that someone with 'evil eyes' puts on a person."

"Oh," I said, wondering what evil spell was put on my mother and by whom.

About nine months later, my mother returned home from the hospital with a baby girl. After three boys in a row, my parents were "just thrilled to finally have a baby girl in our family."

As for me, I didn't give the arrival of the new family member another thought. That is, until Enzo told me that his mom, upon hearing about the birth of new baby sister, said "Well, well, well, the malocchio lady did her magic again."

6.
To Dib or Not to Dib

Moses Abraham.

My special relationship with Moses started from a simple act of kindness to his father and developed into a lasting one through the neighborhood's "dibbing" custom. Now to be clear, Moses was not part of my daily group of friends and I wasn't part of his. His inner group consisted of his older brother, Mustafa, and two neighbors, Omar and Elias Ali. Their fathers, Mr. Abraham and Mr. Ali, were from Syria, the only two such families in the Park.

My dad told me that Mr. Abraham was a mustard-gas casualty of World War 1. He truly was a dead man walking. Every warm spring and summer day, he would slowly shuffle, trance-like, from his house on 24th Street through the connecting alley to 25th Street to watch us kids play our street games of basketball or football. He would stand on the corner of the sidewalk and stare at us while we played. He never talked or showed any outward signs of emotion---he just stood for hours and stared, his eyes fixed and blank. After a while, he became invisible to us kids.

It bothered me that I never saw Mr. Abraham sitting. So, one day I placed a wooden crate from Goldberg's grocery store against a shaded wall and had him sit on it. Somehow, his son Moses, who was a few years older than me, found out about it and went out of his way to find and thank me. From that time on he was especially friendly to me and became one of my regular "dibbers."

But let me back up and briefly tell you about the "dibs" custom in the Park.

Here is how it went: Say I left my house eating one of my mother's delicious homemade Italian donuts. Say Squirt would see me and call out "dibs." Under the rules, I would have to give Squirt a bite of my donut. Of course, if I was worried that he might take a humongous bite, I could break off a small piece of the donut and hand it to him. But the point is, I would have to share the donut under the "dibs" rule. And, if two or more of your buddies hollered "dibs," you might not get to eat very much of "your" donut.

Like all rules, however, there was an exception that went like this: if you saw your friend first you quickly shouted "no dibs" and he would have no claim or right to whatever you were eating. So, the process of "no dibbing" quickly became an art form in the Park. You learned quickly to either look outside first before leaving the house, or you hid what you were eating behind your back, and yelled "no dibs" before anyone could see it.

Of course, you could always opt to eat your cannoli, popsicle, or whatever, in your house, but that was not any fun. Somehow, it always tasted better if you shared it with your inner circle of friends. I rarely "no dibbed" any of my close friends---just the other kids in the Park.

As mentioned earlier, "dibbing" is how Moses and I developed a special relationship. It was as simple as that. Each Friday he would leave his house and offer me a chunk of his mom's freshly-baked flat, round, Syrian bread. Although all of our mothers baked bread, Mrs. Abraham's bread was different in shape and taste. It was deliciously unique and I always looked forward to Friday afternoon around 2:00 when I would meet Moses with a stick of Italian pepperoni. We would sit on the corner curb eating pepperoni wrapped in warm, flat, Syrian bread and loving it to the last bite.

Moses and I remained "dibbers" for a long time.

7. The Clark Bar and the Binoculars

THE CLARK BAR

"Say 10 Our Fathers and 10 Hail Marys" instructed Father Rossi after I confessed. Absolved of my sins, I grabbed the black curtain, pulled it aside, and stepped out of the dark confessional "sweat box."

But, let me start from the beginning.

Squirt and I were sitting on a corner curb waiting for our buddies to come out after dinner when we spotted James walking up our side of 25th Street eating a candy bar. So, we screamed "Dibs." He laughed at us and kept walking by flashing and waving the bar. "Sorry guys, but didn't you hear me call out no dibs." As happened quite often in the Park, because he was older, bigger, and stronger than us, he could get away with lying and not playing by the rules.

"I know it was a Clark bar," said Squirt, "I recognized the wrapper, bright orangish-red with blue letters that spell C L A R K. That's my favorite candy bar."

"Mine, too," I added. "I like it better than a Hershey. God, I wished we had a nickel. Let's go see if we can make some deliveries for Mr. Goldberg."

[Aside: At times, mothers in the Park would order groceries from Goldberg Market over the phone and Mr. Goldberg would pay us a nickel to deliver the "order" to their homes.]

When we reached the store, we were disappointed to hear "there were no orders to deliver." We left and started to walk home. As we turned off Walnut to head up our street, Squirt pulls out a Clark bar. I was shocked. "Where did you …" Well, he shouldn't have but some-how he did so he split the bar in two and we quickly ate it.

We told no one. That is, none of the guys. However, we had no choice but to confess our sin to Father Rossi on Saturday. The good Father told us to tell Mr. Goldberg and pay him for the Clark bar.

"God, what a mess," said Squirt. "Bad enough I had to confess, why did you also confess, I'm the one who stole it."

"But, I ate half and I knew it was stolen. And besides, I didn't want to burn in Hell for a candy bar."

"Well, we are not each going to give him a nickel, it was only one candy bar" said Squirt.

I told Squirt that I just couldn't tell Mr. Goldberg about it. "Neither can I," he said.

"Our parents will be so ashamed and what if Mr. Goldberg calls the police. And you know his son Gilbert will tell everyone at school. What are we gonna do?"

"Don't bring shame to the family name" echoed in my ears.

SO THIS IS WHAT WE DID: We saved five pennies, put them into a sealed envelope, wrote on the front: "Payment in full for one Clark bar" and slipped the envelope into the mail-slot of the front door of Goldberg's Market on Sunday when it was closed and no one was around to see us. Whew, never again.

THE BINOCULARS
Enzo, Alfrado and I were really excited sitting in the grandstands and watching our very first Friday night high-school football game. Two younger boys with

binoculars were sitting next to us. At half-time, Alfrado said he was going to the bathroom. The school band was marching on to the field and Enzo asks one of the boys if he can look through the binoculars to see his girlfriend Ginger, who plays flute in the band.

[Aside: When I heard this, I did a double-take: first, I knew his girlfriend was Rosalie, not Ginger, and second, Rosalie, like us, wasn't in any high-school anything. What is Enzo up to now?]

The boy hands his binoculars to Enzo who looks through it for a minute or so then, OOPS, he drops the binoculars and it falls under the stands. "Oh, sorry," he says, "Wait right here and I'll go under the stands to get it. Come with me, Mair, and help me look." We calmly walk down the rows of seats to the bottom of the stands, go around the side to the back out of sight when Enzo tells me "Let's hurry, Alfrado has the binoculars."

To tell you the truth, I can understand how they tricked the younger kid with the binoculars because they also tricked me.

"We didn't tell you because sometimes you're too much of a goody-goody."

[Aside: For the record, I never, ever, looked through those binoculars---I wanted nothing to do with it. However, I did honor the Park's "code" and never told anyone what happened either.]

"Well, I hope you guys are happy," I said angrily, "now we can't go to any more Friday night high-school games because you know those boys and their parents will be there looking for us."

And we didn't either, not until years later, and, truth be told, I still couldn't totally relax even though we sat on the visiting team's side of the stadium.

8.
FRANNIE

Tonight was a big night and I was excited just thinking about it.

Four of us, Alfrado, Enzo, Augie and I were meeting tonight to play the game of relievo. We heard about relievo from some of the older guys but never played. Frannie, a cute older girl, who was in the 6th grade (we were in the 5th) and pleasingly plump, agreed to play but only with the four of us. No one else. According to Augie, the oldest, we were hand-picked by her. Augie said she liked us, that we were the "good" kids in the Park, and that she trusted us, God forbid, not to tell her mom (who lived alone with Frannie) or anyone else.

Time: After dinner when the corner street light turns on.

Place: Around the corner in the alley where it was dark with a lot of yard-hedges and garden sheds to hide behind.

Rules: Whoever finds Frannie first gets to stay with her and explore a little until Frannie yells "relievo."

Then, that person drops out of the game, goes back to the street corner and waits until the game is finished. Frannie hides again and another one of us finds her, etc… until each of us had his chance to be with Frannie. The game lasts an hour at most, timed to end before our moms start calling us to come home.

When the game ends, we thank Frannie, she giggles, blows us a kiss and hurries home.

We hang around under the corner street lamp to compare notes.

Alfrado says he got to first base, and Enzo says he kissed her and made it "pretty close to second." I say I got a long, tight hug "because I was the youngest and the cutest." And Augie, well he was Augie. He found Frannie last and had been with her the longest before he got his relievo/heave-ho. He wouldn't tell us anything, just kept smiling and shrugging his shoulders.

As we were breaking up to go home, Augie reminded us that if we wanted to play again, we were not to tell anyone except, of course, Fr. Rossi when we went to confession.

In bed that night, I thought of Frannie and our long, tight hug and knew I would love her all my life. I was absolutely positive that she looked at me alone when she blew her kiss.

9.
LITTLE ROBBIE COLE

Nooo! Oh, please God, Nooo! Mrs. Cole's high-pitched screams haunt me still, even after these many years.

I remember it as if it were yesterday. It was Friday, July 2nd, and as planned, I met Enzo at the corner of our street. "You ready for tomorrow morning?" he asked me.

"Yeah, how about you?

"Yeah, the inner tubes are blown up. And my guy Johnnie says he's ready. How about your guy? Is little Robbie ready?"

"Oh yeah," I answered "he's by far the best swimmer of the group. He'll have no problem."

A couple of months earlier, little Robbie Cole and his mother rented a tiny rowhouse at the bottom of my street. One morning I overheard my mother telling a neighbor that Mrs. Cole moved here from Glassport because Robbie "couldn't take it anymore." Seems the boys in his old neighborhood constantly bullied him because he was "different."

Saturday, July 3rd, the morning of Christy Park's annual rite of passage event.

Middle school kids in the Park have been challenged to swim across the Youghiogheny River for as long as anyone could remember. They, like the kids before them, felt they had little choice. The older guys in the neighborhood forced it. Acceptance in the Park only happened if you swam the Yough: "What are you chicken? It's not like we're asking you to swim the Monongahela."

The Yough is about three hundred yards wide, with calm water and a slow current. In truth, the only difficult part to cross is its channel, about thirty yards wide, where the current typically is cold, rough, and quick.

I met Enzo, Johnnie, and Robbie at the bottom of the street where they were waiting. Enzo gave me one of the two inflated inner tubes. We crossed Walnut, then the railroad tracks, and then walked the path along the steel mill's chain-linked fence and down the river bank to Bare-Ass Beach. As we walked, I asked Robbie if he had breakfast and if he was ready. He said he was too nervous to eat and that "he just wanted to get it over with."

We waded into the river as far as we could and then started to swim. The water was warm and calm. Perfect.

The older guys were leading the way, swimming with ease. The seven younger guys were all doing fine.

Enzo, pushing an inner tube in front of him as he swam, reminded Johnnie to pace himself and to stay near the tube. I swam along-side Robbie and kept my tube within his reach.

All was going well until we entered the cold water of the channel. Suddenly, Johnnie yelled out that his legs were cramping. He started to panic and screamed for help. Enzo quickly closed the gap between them and gave him the inner tube to float on. When I heard Johnnie scream, I instinctively turned my head towards him. When I saw he was safe, I turned my head back to see Robbie. He was nowhere to be seen. "Where's Robbie?" I shouted. The older guys quickly swam over to help. Time and time again we dove under the dirty, murky water feeling about for Robbie. After searching for some time, we swam across to the other side of the river. We were all in shock running frantically up and down the river bank looking for any sign of him.

No one heard Robbie cry out.

No one saw Robbie go under.

No one saw little Robbie Cole again.

10.
BARE-ASS BEACH

We kids in the Park learned about guy-stuff and juicy neighborhood gossip by hanging out at our "pool."

Our "pool" was the Youghiogheny River and its muddy shoreline. It had a three-foot high platform made from railroad ties (logs) "borrowed" from the B&O Railroad's open storage depot on 29th Street. The top of the platform was floored with plywood we scrounged from our fathers' cellars and it provided us with a fun place to jump off into the cold river water. And when the river rose after heavy rainstorms, we could actually dive from it.

The Yough was the "perfect" place to cool off during the hot summer months. Well, to be honest, "perfect" is somewhat of an exaggeration. For the steel mills along the river dumped their chemical waste into it daily, so that when we came up from under water, we always had orange-sulphur markings on our chins. Worse yet, there were times when trash and human waste floated by as we were swimming. But, we quickly learned to splash-wave it away and to keep on swimming.

We called our pool Bare-Ass Beach because we skinny-dipped---none of us wore a bathing suit.

We spent a lot of time at the pool because we were free to do as we pleased---there were no girls, parents, or other grownups to tell us what to do. It was a place to learn about sex stuff by asking the older guys a lot of things we couldn't ask our parents.

And we'd hear juicy neighborhood gossip. Like Miss Jane Allen, Frank Furillo's pretty young steelworker boarder, was no longer returning home to Mt Lebanon every weekend. Or the rumor that Lanny Blazza, the good-looking "numbers" guy from the local poolhall, was collecting more than gambling money from widow Mrs. Catore as he made his morning rounds of the numbers-playing-ladies in the neighborhood.

[Aside: I remember how excited my mother got ("Don't tell your father") when she "hit" the numbers: she won $300 on a 2-cent bet she placed with Lanny on the number 444, our house number. Playing numbers daily with Lanny was serious business with the ladies: they all bought "Lucky Number Dream Books," which provided them with a "hot number" to bet based on the subject of their dreams.]

Yeah, the rich kids in Grandview had their swimming pool but we had Bare-

Ass Beach, our learning center away from school. We lived there every summer---until the little Robbie Cole tragedy struck and the police shut it down and made it off limits.

11.
SURVIVAL OF THE FITTEST

Christy Park had a number of bullies who paralyzed us kids, the worst of whom came in the form of a big, strong, teenager named Eugene Borvlik, who lived with his welfared-widowed mother on Walnut Street near the railroad tracks.

Big Gene got away with doing what he wanted. He was pure evil. Always picking on little kids, beating them up "because he felt like it", lying, stealing, skipping school and driving his poor mom to tears because he was always causing trouble.

He was short and stocky with Popeye-type arms, a huge round face with small mean-staring dark eyes, and a mouth that curved slightly downward at its ends that always made him look angry. He was scary-looking and we ran away or hid when we saw him coming.

And he would say strange and scary stuff like: "I'm so strong I can knock myself out."

"Huh?"

I once saw Gene pouring gasoline on a cat, setting it on fire with a match, and laughing as it streaked screeching down Kountz Alley. It was sickening to see.

Another time, he spied Enzo and I walking through the cow pasture on Mr. Gozdik's farm on our way to Bare-Ass Beach. We tried to run away but we saw him too late. He caught Enzo, put his neck in an arm-lock, then picked up some cow dung and smeared it over Enzo's face. When I screamed at him to stop he told me to mind my own business. And when Enzo swore at him, he told Enzo "now big mouth, you are going to eat it" forcing the dung into his mouth. Enzo started throwing up while crying and Gene walked away laughing. Like a typical bully, he only bullied smaller, weaker kids in the Park or ones, like Enzo, who had no brothers. He never bullied me because he knew my older brother Carmen would seek and destroy him if he messed with me.

Survival of the fittest got tested in the Park with Gene around. And poor little Robbie Cole was one who did not make it. Gene tormented Robbie every time he caught him coming home from school. He would force him to do things in an alley behind a garage. Robbie's mom told Mrs. Borvlik about her son's constant bullying of Robbie but the only thing that happened was the bullying got worse for him.

And the really tragic part about all of this was that Big Gene, the bully, NEVER GOT HIS DUE.

Well, enough about Gene Borvlik. I recall him with utter disgust and contempt.

12.
THE RESURRECTION

I awakened Saturday morning, looked out the window, and saw tons of snow everywhere. And that meant only one thing: "sled" riding time.

Kid after kid poured out of his house anxious to get started. A bunch of the older guys spent the next half-hour getting the street ready: hauling bushels of ashes from the back-alleys of our homes and spreading them at the bottom of our hilly street to stop us from sledding into the busy traffic on Walnut. (In those days, all of our homes were heated by coal furnaces so there were plenty of ashes available in the Park.)

Now you should know that no one owned a real sled. Our "sleds" consisted of 3x5-foot flat corrugated metal sheets salvaged from the nearby mills. They were wickedly fast but difficult to control---steering was best achieved by holding on to the sides and leaning our bodies (toboggan style) to whatever direction we wanted to go. And go we did, dodging parked cars, fire hydrants, corner drain sewers, and, at times, incoming traffic.

When we reached the ash-bottomed street, we then carried the sheets over our heads back to the top of the hill to repeat the ride. That was the drill for years until …

Hank Silva's face was sliced open by the metal edge of the sheet he was carrying up the hill. His legs were suddenly hit by a runaway "sled" shooting down the street and his "sled" flew in the air and caught his face. I was the first to reach the spot where he lay. When I saw the side of his face flipped open like a book in the blood-reddened snow, I remember only that I fainted. Fortunately, others ran for help.

For years after the accident, Hank wouldn't attend school or leave his house. He was ashamed to be seen. His older brother, Vinnie, told us his face was all covered with stitches "and looked like picture-puzzle pieces." Local surgeons had operated on him a number of times trying to restore his face to a state of some normalcy. But, truth be told, there simply was not enough money to engage a surgeon skilled in plastic surgery.

Typically, our parents did what they could to help. Money was collected, dinners were prepared and sent to the house, and countless novenas (prayers said nine consecutive days) were said by the Catholic mothers in the Park asking St Jude to help Hank.

And Miss Benson, Hank's 5th grade teacher at Eleventh Ward, stopped by his house every day after school to drop off and pick up his assignments.

To us kids, it was like Hank had died---we never saw him after the accident.

That is, until years later, when his brother Vinnie purchased a ticket for the first-ever Pennsylvania State Million Dollar Lottery. And, yes, you guessed it, despite odds of winning being something like a zillion to 1, Vinnie's ticket was among the winners. What happened next was beautiful. Hank was flown to a special hospital in Boston where a "famous" plastic surgeon successfully operated on him.

When Hank returned home, he finally left his house.

Hank Silva had risen from the dead.

13.
AMEN

At the close of Sunday's ten o'clock Mass, Father Rossi announced his need for altar boys for next year. He made it clear that he expected each of the parish's neighborhoods to be represented. Enzo and I looked at each other and gulped as our mothers smiled and nodded our way. We immediately sensed we were in trouble.

On the long bus ride home, our mothers were glowing with the excitement that one of us might be chosen by the good Father for the honor of serving Mass with him. Enzo and I quickly suggested Augie as the best candidate since he was the oldest.

"Oh no," Enzo's mother said, "age has nothing to do with it. You two as well as your friends will all have to try out for it." My mother, of course, shook her head in full agreement.

The next week was particularly stressful. Each evening, our parents put pressure on us by talking on and on about how important it was for a Christy Parker to finally serve as an altar boy. In the past, St Perpetua's altar boys were chosen exclusively from students who attended the Catholic school near the church.

Walking home from school that week, Enzo, Alfrado, Augie, and I talked about who among us would like the "job."

[Aside: "Lucky" Squirt was home free because he "was some type of Protestant."]

"I would like to do it" lied Alfrado "but, honestly guys, I'm afraid I might let loose with a loud long toot during Mass."

"Oh no, nice try Alfrado" said Augie "but we know you have total control of your tooting."

Alfrado was not about to change his mind. "No way, I'm sorry," he continued, "I'm not going to put on that white dress during Mass, no way."

"It's not a dress," I said, "My dad told me it's called a cassock."

"I don't care what it's called, it still looks like a dress to me," said Alfrado.

"Well, I'm not worried about getting picked," added Enzo, "I don't know all those Latin words, or when to stand, or kneel, or when to ring those little bells, so I feel safe. I am positive that Father Rossi won't pick me."

"I'm out of the running also," said Augie, "I have to baby sit my little sister so my mother can attend Mass. She represents our family on Sundays."

"So that leaves you, Mair. And Father Rossi knows your dad attended the seminary in Italy so you are a shoo-in."

"Ah, come on you guys, I don't want the "job" either. And, you know we don't have a choice. Our parents will insist that we go and do our best at Saturday's tryout. What are we going to do?"

"Well," offered Alfrado, "as Miss Benson always says, let's put on our thinking caps and decide on a Parker who will clearly out-religious any of us."

We then started to recite the names of the Catholic kids living on each street until we reached those living on 27th Street and heard the name: Leo Zappeto.

Leo Zappeto. Yep, Leo's perfect, we agreed. He attends Mass every Sunday. He's also scary smart, neat, doesn't cuss, and the teachers all love his manners.

"And he still wears his first communion scapular around his neck, I saw it in gym class," added Augie.

And so our plan was set.

Leo was ecstatic when he heard we agreed that he would be the best one to represent Christy Park. "Ever since the good Father announced it last Sunday" he confessed "I've been studying the prayers and stuff in my missal to be ready for Saturday's tryouts."

SATURDAY TRYOUTS FOR ST PERPETUA ALTAR BOYS

Father Rossi thanked us for coming and told us that he wanted one altar boy and a backup to represent our neighborhood. He said that whomever he selected would have an experienced altar boy acting as his mentor for the first two or three Sundays so we were not to worry about what to do and when while Mass was going on. "Just follow his lead and do what he does." He then began his questioning.

Alfrado, Enzo, and I were determined to make sure that Leo was selected.

So when Father Rossi asked: What is the most important part of Mass, Alfrado replied "When the basket is passed?"

We nervously waited to see the good Father's reaction and were relieved when we saw him smile and say "Yes, it's important that the Church be financially supported by its parishioners, but the offertory is not the most important part."

Leo then quickly offered: "I think it is when you, Father, turn the bread and wine into the body and blood of Jesus and we receive communion."

Father Rossi nodded his approval and then asked "Tell me, do you know how many readings from the Bible take place at Mass?"

Leo hurriedly answered "three, the last being the gospel" and, once again, the good Father smiled his approval.

We were on a roll, our plan was working.

He then asked me what the explanation of the gospel reading was called. I said I didn't know and guessed "lecture" and he said it was called a "homily" or a "sermon." And, he added "the purpose of the homily is to explain the meaning of the gospel and then to relate it to the lives of the parishioners."

He continued to ask questions for another twenty minutes or so asking us about the rites of communion, the prayer of peace, etc., and we made sure that Leo answered most of them.

Finally, he wrapped up the session by asking us what our favorite part of Mass was, to which Enzo quickly replied: "When you say Mass is over, go in peace." We all nervously laughed, and, once again, were relieved when we saw a smile of understanding on the face of the good and kind Father.

He then said his selections would be announced in Sunday's church bulletin and he thanked us again for attending the tryouts.

On our bus ride home, we felt confident that our plan worked and each of us congratulated Leo.

And, as promised, Sunday's bulletin announced the names of his selections for each neighborhood. For our neighborhood, it listed:

REPRESENTING CHRISTY PARK
Hank Silva---Altar Boy
Leo Zappeto----Backup

"HANK SILVA. What!!! How did that happen, he didn't even show up for the tryouts?"

When I got home, I learned that my father had confided to Father Rossi that Hank had asked him "to please tell the good Father that he really wanted to represent the Park as an altar boy as a way of thanking God for answering all the novenas said for his recovery and also for letting his brother win the State lottery."

After I passed this scoop on to the guys and we thought about it, we all agreed, even Leo, that Hank was an excellent choice to represent Christy Park. Amen.

14.
PAYDAYS

Paydays---the best of times, the worst of times.

Before going home on payday, a lot of the dads stopped off for a few beers at the local beer garden, conveniently located outside the mill entrance on Walnut Street. We kids would wait patiently until our dads came out because we knew that we could ask and get 25 cents to catch the latest Saturday movie matinee. God, how I loved paydays.

The day after payday I would make two trips with envelopes. The first one was through the tunnel under the railroad tracks to the U.S. Steel Company office to "make the monthly payment on our house." I liked doing it because I felt important and grownup and also because I got a free all-day Sugar Daddy sucker from Mrs. Kolodney, who worked in the office. Then, I would head up Walnut Street to Goldberg's Market to pay off our monthly food bill and Mr. Goldberg would give me my favorite candy bar, a five- cent Clark bar. God, how I loved paydays.

[Aside: Mr. Goldberg's son Gilbert was in my class. He was nice, middle-of-the-class smart, slightly overweight, played no sports, and never, ever, came out after school to play. He simply was invisible after school. We often wondered, but never asked, what Gilbert did in his free time.]

Well, to return to my recollection of paydays, there was the beautiful Miss Janet DiMartini. World War II was going on and everyone was contributing to the war effort, including lady steelworkers.

"Rosie the Riveter" posters were displayed everywhere. Many of these lady steelworkers were from small towns around Pittsburgh so they would rent a room in Christy Park to live in during the work-week and then return home on the weekend. Miss DiMartini rented a room in my house. My mom and dad made it clear to me that her room was off limits. She was always listening to music on the radio in her bedroom after dinner. On paydays, she would dress up, meet another lady steelworker or two, and go out dancing in a downtown night club. I tried to stay awake until she came home (not exactly sure why) but I always fell asleep. God, how I wished I was older.

One payday, after dinner, my dad went to the Italians Sons & Daughters of America Lodge and my mom went to visit a sick neighbor. As usual, music was playing in Miss DiMartini's room so I knocked on her door and asked if she needed anything, like "maybe a glass of ice water?" She opened the door, looked at me and smiled, and said no thanks but asked if I knew how to dance. She was dressed in a shiny black dress and looked like a movie star. I remember getting so flustered that I told her "I just love dancing but I don't know to do it." She said she would show me, kicked off her heels, put her arm around me, and started to teach me in the upstairs hallway. A slow song was playing on her radio and I was melting out of her arms and onto the floor like a figure in a Salvador Dali painting. I really don't remember anything else except wishing I were older and could go out dancing with her. When my mom returned home, she asked if Miss DiMartini had left and "hoped that I hadn't bothered her in her room." I said I hadn't, which was the truth. God, how I loved paydays.

Unfortunately, paydays were sometimes not so lovable. Some of the dads stayed at the beer gardens too long. Drank too much and spent too much. Worried moms would tell their sons to "go bring their dads home." Sometimes that worked, but there were also times when a father would get somewhat violent and scream at his son "to go back home if he knew what was good for him." Hours later, his son would get a couple of us kids to go with him to help bring his drunken dad home. Still, at other times, a frantic mom, worried about the rent or mortgage, would have no choice but to walk down to Walnut Street and ask another adult neighbor standing on the corner to go into the beer garden and tell her husband she was outside. More times than not, the scene that followed was ugly and sad: first there was the dad hollering and cussing, then the mom pleading with him, and finally, the embarrassed mom would go home alone sobbing and ashamed.

God, how I hated those paydays.

15.
The Foreigner

One Saturday morning around 10 o'clock Augie came running out of his house to tell Enzo, Squirt, and me that our neighbor Mr. Furillo had died last night.

"Oh God, not another funeral," we said.

"How did he die?" we asked Augie.

Augie, who was always the first to hear the news in the neighborhood, told us that the rumor was he died in his bed doing his "marriage duty."

"How do you die from that?" asked Enzo.

"Boy if you can die from that I'm never getting married." added Squirt.

"Look," I said smugly, "you can die from anything, and at any time. That's why you always have to be in a state of grace."

"Oh, God," said Augie to me, "there you go again sounding like Father Rossi."

"Listen, Augie," Enzo said "why don't we ask your brother Paulie about it. Is he home?"

"Yep, he's home, he's working the 3 to11 shift, let's go ask him."

Paulie was in the back yard sitting under the grape-arbor trellis drinking coffee and reading the Daily News sport pages. When we asked him to explain the rumor of Mr. Furillo's death, Paulie told us to ask our fathers. We reminded him that our fathers were working the early shift.

(Our dads had plant seniority and worked the best shift—7 a.m. to 3 p.m.)

So, Paulie explained how a husband could die from doing his "marriage duty." "Listen, when you get married you have the duty to provide food, clothing, and a place to live for your wife and children. So, you have to work hard and long. And Mr. Furillo had been working for over 20 years in the mill. He had a hard job and he probably came home dead tired, fell on his bed to rest, and just died. Trust me, it's sad but it happens. Now, go play and let me read the paper in peace."

"Okay, thanks Paulie," we yelled as we ran off to play.

The funeral rituals in the Park typically involved loud outbursts of grief at the cemetery by the new widows. They would sob uncontrollably, scream out the husband's name, faint, hurl their bodies on the coffin and hug it, and attempt to jump into the gravesite after the coffin was lowered. As for the jump, it never in fact happened because the sons or daughters would stand along the sides of their mother and hold her arms tightly to prevent her from actually jumping into the grave. Now, don't get me wrong, it was real grief being displayed but the wailing of the widows was so sad and scary to us kids that we only went to funerals when required by our parents.

And we were forced to go to Mr. Furillo's funeral.

Ms. Jane Allen was 18 years younger than Frank, who was a widower when they met. She was a pretty steelworker who rented a room in his house during the war, fell in love with Frank, married, and never returned to her home in Mt Lebanon, a white-collar suburb of Pittsburgh.

Frank Furillo's Funeral: After the mass at St Perpetua's, Mrs. Jane Allen Furillo, family members, and neighbors caravanned to the Italian cemetery for burial. We all joined in Fr Rossi's prayers for Mr. Furillo's soul, shoveled some dirt on the lowered casket, and left. The ceremony was serene and respectful, unlike any Park funeral any of us had witnessed. We liked it---it was like the funerals we saw in the movies. Sad but nice.

But it only took about two weeks afterwards before the female tongues started to wag in the Park.

"Did you hear Jane Furillo was seen walking to catch the bus on Walnut Street and she was not dressed in black."

[Aside: A Christy Park widow typically wore all black for a year: black dress, black stockings, black shoes, black hat, black veil, --- and no makeup. And she was expected to stay at home to pray the rosary and receive neighbors during the year grieving period.]

"And she was seen wearing red lipstick."

"And Mrs. Cirello saw her last week at the Memorial movie theater downtown."

"And Mrs. Martino went to the house to drop off some lasagna and she came to the door wearing a loud red and white flowered house dress and the radio could be heard blasting away."

"Yes, and what did you expect, don't forget, at the cemetery she didn't scream out poor Frank's name even once."

"Nor did she even hug or kiss his casket."

"Poor Frank, he was such a good man. He'd be so ashamed if he were alive."

"He deserved better."

Blah, blah, blah, as the tongues wagged on and on until …

To the surprise of no one in Christy Park, a month after Frank was buried, Widow Jane Allen Furillo sold her house and moved back to Mt. Lebanon.

"Well, what did you expect" chorused the ladies of the Park "That's what happens when a Christy Parker marries a foreigner."

16.
THE FIGHT

The bell rang and Mrs. Cooper dismissed us from her 6th grade classroom. Alfrado, Enzo, and I grabbed our books and headed home. As usual, we headed down 29th Street, then took the first right turn on to Beale alley heading towards home on 25th.

We were doing the normal after-school moaning and groaning about all the homework Mrs. Cooper assigned for tomorrow, when we saw a group of girls waiting for us to catch up to them.

Before we could even say Hi, Rosalie Cameroli, Enzo's "steady," ran up to him and hollered: "Is it true that you walked Delores home from school on Monday?"

Enzo smiled and said "Yeah, but it was no big deal, Rose, everyone knows you're my girlfriend."

"Yes," snapped Rosalie, "everyone but you and Delores, it seems" and she angrily shoved Enzo to the ground. Enzo's books went flying and Rosalie's friends all cheered their approval.

[Aside: Fights between boys in the Park were common. But in all my years there, that is the only time I saw or even heard of one involving a girl and a boy.]

But back to the fight. At first, Enzo was somewhat embarrassed and tried to laugh it off, but that only made Rosalie madder. As they say in the Park, "she was hotter than a blast furnace." She started kicking him and hitting him with her fists and, when he covered himself with his arms to protect himself while on the ground, she grabbed and yanked his hair. All of the other girls were egging her on "to teach that two-timer a lesson."

She kept punching with both hands until he finally stood up and yelled "That's enough."

That did it. Rosalie immediately stopped punching and, somewhat exhausted, started to cry. "And you better not cheat on me again or else" she hollered over her shoulder as she walked away with her friends.

Truth be told Alfrado and I were shocked by what we saw. It was a side of Enzo we had never seen. For throughout the Park, he had a reputation that he was not to be messed with ever since he backed down the Park's biggest bully, Eugene Borvlik. Once, when Gene tried to bully him, he got a weird-wild look in his eyes, then grabbed a brick and dared Gene to take another step towards him and "he'd crush his skull." Enzo's face was white and he was shaking with anger like a mad man. All of us guys who witnessed the scene saw Gene back off and heard him say "he was only kidding." After that incident, word quickly spread through the Park and no one messed with "crazy Enzo." Yet, here he was taking a pretty good licking from Rosalie without doing anything.

So, we helped Enzo pick up his scattered books. "Why didn't you defend yourself?" asked Alfrado. "Yeah," I added, "Rosalie made you look like a sissy. You know it will be all over the school tomorrow that you were beaten up by a girl."

"Ah, I don't care about that. And, besides, she was right. She's my steady and I shouldn't have cheated on her. I'll apologize to her tomorrow morning when I stop by her house to walk her to school."

"Wow," said Alfrado, shaking his head in disbelief at what he just heard, "I'm never going to go steady with any girl," and for emphasis, he punctuated his remark by lifting his right leg and letting loose a long loud toot.

With that, we all just cracked-up laughing and started walking home.

[Aside: Alfrado's quick release of toots was well known among his friends; his toots were like bullets on a cowboy's gun-belt, always ready to be fired.]

17.
S.L.

Generation after generation of families lived in the same houses in Christy Park--- a new family moving in the Park was a rare event. So, when it happened, as it did at the beginning of my seventh-grade school year, the news quickly rippled through the neighborhood.

"Wow," said Augie as he approached a bunch of us guys on the corner, "guess what, a new family just moved into the Tucci house at the top of our street. "And gentlemen," he said excitedly, "wait 'til you feast your eyes on their daughter. She is different from any of the girls in the Park. She has blonde hair, blue eyes, and a complexion like Ivory soap. She's very, very pretty."

So, you can imagine my surprise when the next day, Miss Jones, our 7th grade teacher, introduced and welcomed her to our class. "Class, this is our new student, Lori Culbere, who recently moved here from Grandview." The guys went bonkers, looked at Augie and gave him a thumb's up. She was drop-dead pretty and as luck would have it, she was in my class.

Going home after school that day, we guys wondered out loud about which one of us would become her boyfriend.

"Don't forget guys," reminded Augie, "Miss Jones said she's from Grandview."

"Yeah" added Squirt, "where the father's wear white shirts and ties and drive Buicks to work."

"Yeah, but she didn't seem snooty or stuck-up," Enzo said.

The next day we learned from our classmate, Mary Cobana, that Lori's father was the new assistant principal at our school. And that he was going to take Principal Wilson's place when he retired at the end of the school year.

"Well," I added, "I guess that explains why her family moved here."

"And," continued Mary, "they are the renting the Tucci house only until their new house is built on the empty lot at the top of the street."

"Yeah, yeah, Mary," I said impatiently, "but do you have any personal scoops about her?"

"No," replied Mary, "only that she seems very nice and all the girls in the class like her a lot."

The next few weeks of my life were wonderful. I got to know Lori well and walked to and from school with her almost every day. Some days I even carried her books. In fact, we were together so much that my friends began teasing me, saying that she had a crush on me. Truth is, she had become my S.L. (Secret Love).

And when my S.L. invited me to her birthday party, I told Enzo I was going to ask her to "go steady" with me. "Go for it, Mair," he said "I know she likes you."

Augie, Enzo, and Squirt were also invited to her party---as were Mary, Rosalie, and Delores.

The Day of the Birthday Party. As planned, the four of us guys all showed up together. Lori answered the door in a pink party dress and I instantly felt butterflies. Mary and the other girls had already arrived and were seated in the living room. I couldn't wait for the party to begin. (Oh, God, please let the bottle point to me when Lori spins it.) My heart was thumping just thinking about the spin-the-bottle kissing game.

Then it happened: Mrs. Culbere walked into the living room while chatting with a tall, nice-looking, clean-cut guy.

Who the heck was he? I wondered. Didn't have to wonder long: Lori introduced him to us: "I'd like everyone to meet my boyfriend, Will Richards. Will is from my old neighborhood."

As soon as I heard the word "boyfriend," the "party" in birthday party was over for me.

As Enzo and I were walking home afterwards, I was still stunned and somewhat in shock. Why didn't she tell me about him. I didn't say a word as we walked down the street to my house. As I walked up the steps to my front porch, Enzo, who knew me better than I knew myself, asked if I was going to be okay.

"Yeah," I lied. Then I slammed the door, shot up the stairs to my bedroom, flung myself on the bed, and cried until I fell asleep.

***
SPIN THE BOTTLE PARTY GAME
Spin-the-bottle was always the highlight of a party. It was a kissing game that went like this. Each girl would take a turn at spinning an empty milk bottle in the center of a circle of boys. If the neck of the bottle pointed to you when it stopped spinning, then you and the girl would leave the room and kiss if, and only if, both agreed.

18.
TECH OR VOC

I was in the 8th and final grade of my elementary school.

During the last month of school, our teachers and Mr. Culbere, the principal, kept emphasizing to our class the importance of choosing the "right" high school next year. The choices were Technical High School or Vocational High School. Tech High was where you went if you were going to college. Vocational High was where you went to learn a craft to get a job after graduation.

"It will be one of the most important decisions you make," said Miss Judith, our 8th grade teacher. "We here at Eleventh Ward have done our best to prepare you, whether you choose to go to Tech or Voc. Do well, so we can be proud of you. And to help you decide, tomorrow, we will have two of our former students speak to you: one went to Tech and the other went to Voc."

The next morning at school, as promised, a spit and polished, shoulders-back U.S. Army officer was standing in front of the class. His uniform jacket with its insignia patch, colored ribbons, and two shiny silver bars on each of his shoulders was a sight none of us had seen before, except in movies. He said he was Captain Joseph Tassoni and he had attended Tech. He told us he recently had been discharged from the Service and that he would be attending University of Pittsburgh in September on the "G.I. Bill." He spent the next twenty minutes or so telling us about how he became an officer (attended Officer Training School) and how, because he went to Tech and took college prep courses, he qualified for admission into Pitt. He answered our questions and then thanked us and Miss Judith for inviting him.

After lunch, Miss Judith introduced Joseph Glass, who told us that he was working as a machinist for U.S. Steel. He told us that after finishing 8th grade he decided to attend Voc because he liked to "work with his hands and fix things." He said that at Voc he took various industrial classes before deciding he liked making parts to repair machinery the best. He then described his typical workdays at the mill designing and making parts to repair stuff like cranes, bulldozers, and Bessemer converters.

He drew sketches of the machines/equipment etc. on the blackboard and then drew pictures of the parts he made to repair them. "Remember," he added, "Voc offers you many choices, such as plumbing, drafting, and barbering to name a few, any one of which will guarantee you a good-paying job after graduation. I'm living proof of that." He ended his talk by telling us how much he loved what he was doing and how glad he was to have chosen Vocational High.

Walking home after school that day we talked about our futures---it was exciting. Exciting, that is, at least for us guys. The girls were really steamed. "Same old story for us," said Mary, "the best we girls can hope for is to take shorthand and typing, and get an office job in the steel mill."

"Yeah," chimed in Rosalie, "or like our mothers, just finish high school, marry a Christy Parker and raise a family."

"Right," added Delores, "you noticed that both speakers were guys. How depressing is that."

Changing the mood, I said "Can you believe what we heard from Captain Tassoni? At last, someone from Christy Park is going to college. No one, and I mean no one, in the Park has ever gone to college." I was still stunned and couldn't believe it. But, for some reason,

I felt excited and proud. I couldn't wait to get home to tell my mom and dad.

"Yeah, yeah," said Alfrado "but, you like school and even make the honor roll. I don't like school. I can't wait to turn 18 so I can join the Navy and see the world. Heck, I've never even seen downtown Pittsburgh."

"Oh, you just want to join the Navy to eat their beans," joked Squirt.

"I'm going to Voc," Enzo said with determination, "I'd like to be a machinist and get a good-paying job like Joe Glass. Hey, the mill is good enough for our dads so it's good enough for us. Besides our dads can't afford college so going to Tech would be a waste."

"What about you, Augie?" I asked.

"Well, as you guys know, my brothers went to Voc and now work in the mill like my dad, but I'm going to Voc to become a beautician and run my own beauty shop."

"Figures," said Enzo, "you just want to be in class with girls all day." As usual, Augie didn't say anything; he just smiled at Enzo's comment.

"What about me?" asked Squirt. "Doesn't anybody care about what I want to be."

We all answered, "Sorry, Squirt, what do you want to be when YOUUU grow up?"

"I want to be a cop," said Squirt ignoring our tease. "Where do I go to learn to be a cop?"

None of us answered. "Ask Miss Judith tomorrow," Mary volunteered.
"Yeah, good idea," said Squirt, "Miss Judith knows everything."

Halfway home, I dropped out of the conversation, as my mind began to drift:

"I wonder what the University of Pittsburgh even looks like."

Epilogue

Enzo married Rosalie after high school and worked in the steel mill as a rigger. Squirt became a motorcycle cop. Alfrado never joined the Navy, but worked in the mill as a pipe fitter. Mary worked in U.S. Steel's front office. Delores and her mom and dad moved to Ohio. And I, like Captain Tassoni, attended college on the G.I. Bill (Korean).

What about Augie? Well, he was one of Christy Park's nice success stories. He quickly became a "name" hair stylist and his "Fifth Avenue Beauty Salon" overflowed with women customers over the years. Nothing had changed much---the women still loved Augie. Even after his customers died, the local funeral director was told by the families that "their mothers only wanted Augie to fix their hair for their trip to Heaven."

And Augie always did.

Author's Note

The advice of my parents is as relevant today as it was then. Today, there are more than a million new immigrants who are also telling their first-generation American children to do the best they can in school, to respect the laws of our country, and to not shame their family names---time-tested advice that helps keep America great.